*Letter to
a Jewish Friend*

Letter to a Jewish Friend

Ibrahim Souss

Translated by John Howard

Quartet Books
London

First published in English by
Quartet Books Limited 1989
A member of the Namara Group
27/29 Goodge Street, London W1P 1FD

First published in France by
Editions du Seuil 1988
under the title *Lettre à un ami Juif*

British Library Cataloguing in Publication Data

Souss, Ibrahim, *1945–*
    Letter to a Jewish friend.
    1. Palestine. 1945–1985.
    Public opinion in Western World.
    I. Title   II. Lettre à un ami Juif
    956.94′05

    ISBN 0-7043-2703-1

Typeset by AKM Associates, Southall, London
Printed and bound in Great Britain by
The Camelot Press PLC, Southampton

If they should hold their peace,
the stones would immediately cry out.

Luke, xix, 40

We catalogued all the pain the torturer could possibly inflict on every inch of our bodies; then, with anguish in our hearts, we went and faced him.

René Char

'Victory never pays, but every mutilation of man is an unforgivable act,' wrote Albert Camus in his *Letters to a German Friend*, as the Nazi hordes overran Europe. Rereading that sentence, which I had been turning over in my head for a long time, I thought of you. I resolved to write to you, because I remain convinced that the deep meaning of those words won't be lost on you at this critical moment, this turning-point in the story of our interrupted friendship.

Your voice, my friend, has been strangely silent

for some time now, and that hurts me . . . No, I won't beat about the bush. I'll come right to the point, and be as frank as I can. Our relations were always frank.

Since Israeli soldiers have started shooting Palestinian children, your silence has shocked me. I'm not used to it.

And yet I think I can almost understand this reticence, this hesitation. I think I can see in it an expression of that hidden anxiety that grips the hearts of a generation that survived the death camps, each time Israel finds itself confronted with the inescapable dilemma that the Jews have been trying in vain to avoid for forty years. What am I saying? For nearly a century, ever since Theodor Herzl decided to set up a Jewish state in a Palestine inhabited by Arabs.

I can hear you saying that you condemn acts of brutality, and that you regret that the army has opened fire on young demonstrators, but that

2

the violence has to stop on both sides; that the young Palestinians who have thrown stones at Israeli soldiers must also bear some of the responsibility. You must concede that the word 'but' is one word too many in that statement. It's a dangerous word that gives rise to confusion, by blurring the distinction between a victim and his persecutor.

I find it hard to resign myself to the idea that your memory has become so unclear. We agreed in the past, almost tacitly, that the road leading to the coexistence of Arabs and Jews on the soil of Palestine, even though tortuous and strewn with obstacles, was worth exploring. We should never have broken off our dialogue.

I'd like, therefore, to consider this letter an open-ended one. Of necessity, it will be incomplete and unfinished. I won't bring it to an end until the day I make you understand that coexistence implies the defusing, the neutralization of all anxiety.

Do you remember my telling you, after our first meeting, how much sympathy I felt for your people's past suffering?

It was that tragedy which, in part at least, was responsible for my discovering my own identity as a man.

In order to understand a little better, I lost no time in visiting the death camps. I went to Dachau, Bergen-Belsen, Mauthausen, and other sinister places. My flesh felt bruised by the experience; in solidarity, I left a fragment of

4

my soul between the whitewashed crematorium walls.

I wanted to sound the depths of the abyss and walk in the footsteps of your tormentors. I went to Nuremberg and sought out the stadium where frenzied crowds had roared out their hatred. I searched the air for echoes; I seemed to feel the vibrations of those rabid voices, to smell the sweat of those inflamed bodies, to catch a glimpse of those crazed looks.

Do you also remember how I asked you, the day we met, why you looked so astonished? You stammered the word 'Arab'. I told you that I, too, had never seen a Jew before. At least at such close quarters. From the top of the dividing wall in Jerusalem, as a child, I had watched the people walking in the street, now out of bounds to me, where my grandfather's house had been. The first time, I had thought: the Jews are just like us, they aren't the devils constantly conjured up by my scarred memory since that terrible day in May 1948 when, with bombs falling all around us, my family set out on the road to exile. I was much too young to remember clearly, or put an actual physical shape to all the people who had filled my childhood. Some of those people – neighbours, friends of the family – had been Jews.

And when you heard me utter a few words, as if they had been words of reassurance, I read in your eyes: well, well, the Arab (I don't think you yet thought of me as the Palestinian) is just like me. Your memory must have been cluttered with distorted images and misleading clichés.

That day, I expressed to you my conviction that the Palestinians and the Israelis couldn't live forever divided by barbed wire; that the land they shared was too small to be torn apart and parcelled up for long.

I'll let you into a secret I've kept to myself for years: that day, I saw you give a start. Yes, unconsciously, you rejected the idea of a 'shared land'. Deep in your eyes I caught a glimpse of that unspoken rejection: for you, that sacred land could not be shared, could never be shared. But you probably judged that this wasn't the time to raise such an objection, and so you said nothing.

Later, many years later, under different circumstances, you had the same reaction. We were sitting side by side in a lecture hall, listening attentively to a talk given by a brave young Israeli, in which he advocated a shared struggle for a shared future. I felt your forearm twitch, and your muscles tense.

A few minutes later, the Israeli was assaulted by fanatics, and suffered a serious stab wound. It was a miracle that he escaped death.

I'll let you into another secret: as I saw the flash

8

of the knife blade, the thought occurred to me very strongly that the Israelis had a duty to show greater courage than the Jews.

I know you'll be angry when you read those words. Yes, I'm daring to make a distinction. You must be thinking: careful, the enemy's trying to divide our ranks, the ranks of the Jewish people. But you know very well that when I write the word 'courage', I'm not attaching any derogatory connotation to it, I'm not making any reference to your tragic past, as you once accused me of doing.

And I imagine that, since our falling out, you've kept that reflex that I was never able to rid you of, the reflex of self-defence, like the tortoise retreating into its shell at the first sign of danger. Am I wrong? But don't worry, I understand that reflex, it seems to me quite natural, because it was developed collectively . . . But I'll come back to it, just as I intend returning to my conception of a 'Jewish people'.

Anyway, I was talking about courage, a quality the Israelis ought to have demonstrated more conspicuously. I think you'll admit that the generation of Israelis that shoots Palestinian children is not notable for its courage. Isn't it a generation in whom military superiority has bred arrogance and contempt for the Arabs?... No, I'm not trying to provoke you, just to prod your conscience. When for years the slogan 'we must break the bones of the Arabs' has been on Israeli lips, when, more recently, a deliberate policy of beatings is implemented without the slightest hesitation, I don't think you can escape the conclusion that the Arabs, and especially the Palestinians, are in the process of becoming *Untermenschen* for a large percentage of Israeli opinion. Notice I don't say 'Jewish' opinion. All the same, I'm convinced that the Jews are gradually losing their 'soul', that agonized but clear conscience that illuminated a whole aspect of human history. Why? Well, quite simply because the spilling of children's blood by the military should never be tolerated, under any circumstances. Yet this time, you have to admit, the reaction hasn't been like that at all. With a few rare exceptions, the voice of the Jewish conscience, your voice, has not been raised, when it ought to have rung out loud and clear to exorcize the demons that have been reawakened.

Believe me, my friend. I'm speaking to you in all sincerity. This Israel that you Jews have given birth to will quickly become a cancer, first eating away at the edges of your collective ego, then attacking its essence, if you don't take urgent action. You must scold your children. And when I say scold, I mean punish severely. At once, before it's too late.

The wounds of the Palestinian people are open and gaping; the more time passes, the harder it will be to treat them.

Don't stand there doing nothing, saying nothing.

Remember your father's suffering, and act quickly.

Why do you hesitate? Don't tell me, I can guess.

And yet you admit that it hurts to see Israeli soldiers *forced to open fire. But what can Israel do, with its very existence threatened*? And in the same breath, you assert that you love Israel deeply, but that you are undergoing a terrible trauma and you need understanding.

I'm overcome by a tremendous sadness: you've changed profoundly since we stopped seeing each other. Has the circle of those you love shrunk until it has become a narrow coterie, to which you've decided only your 'co-religionists' can be admitted?

How could Israel's existence be threatened,

when it maintains the strongest armed forces in the region, when it's a fully-fledged member of the planet's nuclear club, and when fighter-bombers carrying the Star of David sow terror in Arab towns, villages and camps?

You say it hurts you to see Israel in such a position, but what's the alternative? As inconceivable as it may seem, aren't you simply turning a deaf ear to the voice of your conscience, that conscience which was formed in the pain of the death camps, and which, by definition, can't be eroded, even by self-interest?

Let me refer once again to the anxiety you feel for Israel. I understood it that day we were together on a train and you showed me that sinister number tattooed on your arm. That's why I tolerate your indecision, your hesitation, your prevarication, even though the State of Israel has taken everything from me: my house, my garden, my flag, my passport, the graves of my ancestors. And what is more, I'm holding out my hand once again, because there are two things this State, in its deadly fury, has not been able to take from me, will never be able to take from me, two things which have remained

15

deep inside me: my dignity and my conscience.

And I'm going to suggest what we can do next, if you give me the chance, if you grasp the olive branch, if you condescend to speak to me. Yes, I suggest we speak to each other, we resume the dialogue we broke off when you could no longer bear to hear me talk about my homeland.

Order your brothers to lay down their arms.

Together, we can build a shared future. Together, we'll be able to tell our children that we managed to overcome our mutual anxieties.

Don't hesitate any longer! Turn aside your soldiers. Protect our children with your body.

I've understood your anxiety. Now it's your turn to consider mine. I invite you to join me in exorcizing them together. They are not insurmountable.

Isn't the killing of children, or any kind of killing, an admission of impotence? Aren't violence, bombings, the endless waging of war a kind of quicksand, into which those who persecuted you in the past hope that you will sink?

This is a cry from the heart that I'm addressing to you. There is an existential dilemma facing your people, and now is the time to meet it head on.

Israel can no longer ignore the choice implicit

in its having taken root in the land of Palestine. Sooner or later, it will have to become part of the Middle East, while keeping its own individual character.

In my view, that's the only way for the Jews to preserve intact their identity and the age-old traditions that they guard so jealously. To wage war without end is to choose the option of self-destruction, the option chosen by Samson when he cried with rage: 'Let me die with the Philistines!' before shaking the pillars of the temple, and bringing it down on his head and on the heads of everybody present.

For a whole evening, once, we argued about the concept of 'nationhood', and whether the criteria for it should be objective or subjective.

Didn't Stalin ratify the objective approach when he ordered that the records of all Soviet Jewish citizens should carry, next to their nationality, an indication of their religious affiliation?

You had Marxist leanings in those days, and you tried to convince me that the Stalinist idea was the right one. I resisted, because I tended to regard all nationalism as a relic of times past. Don't forget that the Jews were responsible in my eyes for all the suffering my people had experienced. Nevertheless, I overcame my understandable gut reaction (which was also an intellectual reaction) and replied that, in my opinion, the Jews were a people *from the moment they subjectively considered themselves a people*.

You immediately parried: 'And are the Israelis a people?' with that ironic expression on your face that you always have whenever you forget you're dealing with a friend. I didn't answer you. I evaded your question because I wasn't sure of my response. You didn't insist, but I could see a glint of triumph in your eyes. It didn't bother me for the good reason that, unsure as I was of my response, I didn't doubt that I would be morally capable of moving to a position where I could one day grant recognition to my enemy, once I had gained the necessary conviction. Besides, that evening, the question didn't seem to me of paramount importance.

What I really wanted to talk about was anxiety. I wanted to reassure you, to tell you again that I understood the fear that your forebears had felt deep in their souls. I wanted you to know that I was the first to proclaim out loud that the whole of humanity had to bear responsibility for the terrible legacy of the Nazis. Including us, the Palestinians, not because we were directly or indirectly implicated – we are innocent of the blood of your martyrs – but because we were perfectly well aware that, in order to prevent the 'unclean beast' from ever rising up again to threaten you, or us, or all mankind, vigilance had to become part of our collective consciousness, had to be imprinted, as it were, in the genes of every human being.

I told you we were prepared to assume that legacy, and you stared at me, stunned and incredulous, and asked me if there were any conditions attached to that standpoint. I replied that for that assumption of responsibility to become possible, the conduct of those Jews who had settled on the soil of Palestine would have to be exemplary. Above suspicion.

We would have to be protected from the accusations our children would be sure to level at us if they observed the slightest weakness. Please understand me. We have no right to involve our children in an awareness of your past suffering, with all the mass of collective guilt it will generate, if you lack rigour with regard to your own people. For the demons I referred to are not selective. They can appear in any man, any group, even Jews.

I had dared to hope that the sufferings of the Jews would have made them immune; the majority of Israelis have proved to me that I was wrong. I think you have to admit that what is now being inflicted on the Palestinians is also persecution, also a crime. I can hear you muttering that there's no comparison. But suffering, my friend, knows no boundaries, either in time or space.

When a Palestinian mother weeps for her son, murdered by a settler, her grief fills the whole of space, it spreads out to infinity, it rends the sky. For her, the young man she has lost is equal to all the men in the world.

That's valid for me and, I think, having looked deep into your soul, for you, too. That's why your silence wounds me; that's why the few statements of yours that have been reported to me by mutual friends are hardly more eloquent than your silence, as long as you haven't dared accept responsibility for the sufferings of the Palestinians.

There's a quality that for a long time I hoped to find in you, a quality that would have appealed to me and redeemed you in my eyes: tolerance, a tolerance more wide-ranging than has become customary among your people.

But I haven't lost hope. I'll never forget how, one day, you sent a friend of yours to place a spray of flowers on my father's grave, near Bethlehem. You knew that, because of exile, I hadn't been there when he had breathed his last, and I hadn't been able to close his eyelids. You confided to me how uneasy you felt. You whispered: could these flowers make up for those wrongs?

I thought then that you were on your way to rediscovering the truth, the truth bequeathed to you by your ancestors. You averted your eyes when I looked at you, for fear that I would detect the smallest chink in the armour of your conscience.

That day, I felt hope.

A friend of yours recently wrote that Yiddish poetry invents for us a thousand and one ways to be a Jew, 'because to be a Jew is to be a mirror of the whole of mankind, a shattered mirror, perhaps, broken by centuries of dispersal and alienation, but a mirror where we see, constantly reconstructed, the persistent image of one of the most intense human experiences of resistance to Time. To be a Jew, in fact, is to find in oneself that which makes one different from, and similar to, every other person.'*

I'd say that the Palestinian poetry I introduced you to was almost exactly the other side of the same coin. But why have I suddenly mentioned poetry? Because I'd also like to talk to you about the earth. The earth of my homeland that my feet no longer have the right to tread. And also because I must tell you how we were deprived of our birthright. How the deeds to our houses, our lands, our entire heritage, were rendered invalid, simply because Israel decided to consider all this property as belonging to absentees. It was routinely confiscated and became the property, first of the Jewish Agency, then of the State. There's no way for us to recover it. There's no court of justice in the world in a position to receive a complaint lodged by a Palestinian. By becoming refugees, we automatically become non-persons. That was your aim; it was what you worked to achieve. But I'll come back to that aspect of our suffering.

---

* Charles Dobzynski, *Le Miroir d'un peuple*, Gallimard, 1971; new revised and expanded edition, in the series 'Domaine yiddish', Editions du Seuil, 1987.

From Fadwa Tuqan to Mahmud Darwish and many others, Palestinian poetry is a reflection of suffering. In its extreme concentration and its profusion of symbols, the only thing it derives from exile and dispersal is the initial experience of suffering; everything else, in both inspiration and expression, has another source, a deep attachment to the earth.

Palestinian thought has found new accents to express an old suffering. It demonstrates a sensibility seared by events but, at the same time, anxious to transcend them through a vision deeply rooted in an acute sense of the human condition, over and above the political tragedy. This gives it an almost mystical transparency; it projects the image of a dis-embodied infinity, but also an ordeal of love suffusing a particular landscape or a particular situation, and expressed with anguished hyper-bole. It is, in fact, the profound contradiction, the fundamental contrast that exists between the image of Jewish 'alienation' – which we see you living through in the land of Palestine –

and the Palestinian vision, that determines the part that poetry plays in the Palestinian revolution. It confirms the fighter in his vocation and shows the extent of his attachment to his land.

It's clear, then, that by offering a sufficiently broad and multi-faceted canvas for the depiction of all the various aspects of Palestinian suffering, poetry faithfully reflects the pain of our existence.

And while the dark years took their course:

I saw you in the sand and the salt of the sea
you were beautiful as the earth, as the children,
as the jasmin
*and I make a vow . . .**

we, too, let out a fierce cry that was the

---

* Mahmud Darwish, 'A Lover of Palestine', *Rien qu'une autre année. Anthologie poétique 1966–1982,* Editions de Minuit, 1983.

expression of *our* resistance to Time:

> *We think of life*
> *with impatience*
> *the time for weeping*
> *is past.**

---

* Idem, 'The Fall of the Moon', *ibid.*

But let me tell you a story. Soon after the war of June 1967 (which the Jews, with pride and contempt, call 'the Six-Day War'), an old friend of our family went to look for his old house in Jerusalem, abandoned like so many others in 1948, so great was the terror spread by the Stern and Irgun groups . . . Don't make that face! There's no point in retorting that nobody had forced our old friend to leave. Between you and me, that's a worn-out argument. Surely you're convinced by now. I've told you about my childhood terror, about my family fleeing before the advance of the armed Zionist gangs.

The same thing happened to all of us . . .

Anyway, this poor man had no difficulty in finding his house. The area had hardly changed. He recognized all the houses of his Muslim and Christian friends, all abandoned.

He hung around outside the house for a long time, then, unable to resist an overwhelming desire to go inside, he took his courage in both hands and rang the bell.

An old man opened the door. He said: '*Shalom.*'

Our friend said: 'This is my house.'

There was a long silence. The two men stared at each other. (All these details were later reported to my father.)

The old man said: 'I know.' He hesitated before adding: 'In 1949, when I came here from Rumania, I had no idea. They told me they'd built these houses especially for us.'

Our friend began to cry. From the half-opened door, he had just caught sight of the old print of Jerusalem which he had hung on the wall a few months before his hurried departure. He said: 'That's my picture.'

The old man turned, and went and took the picture down from the wall. He held it out to him. 'Forgive me.' There were tears in his eyes.

Our friend took the print. He said nothing. He returned home. He told his children never to abandon their land.

Two days later, he died of a heart attack. We assumed his heart had burst with grief.

I'll tell you this. We were deprived of our birthright once, and we've learned our lesson. We won't let ourselves be dispossessed again. We'll lay down our lives if need be.

And I'll tell you something else. That old Rumanian Jew, one of the generation that still bore the scars of the Holocaust, understood. How easy would he find it, today, to convey that understanding to the new generation of conquerors?

The terrible thing about your silence is that it places you, *ipso facto*, among those who refuse to recognize that a certain vision of the future is a dead end. You're probably thinking: Let's allow the Israeli army to do its job and apply the policy of the 'iron fist'. As long as the world makes no move, all resistance will disappear. You're expecting us to stand calmly by and be witnesses to our own destruction. You'd like us to wait with folded arms while Israel instals settlers on what remains of our lands. You're banking on our inertia.

But since 1967, a generation of Palestinians has grown up under military occupation. It has never known how it feels to be independent. It has been humiliated and tortured. Don't you realize that it'll never let itself be crushed?

You're counting on the world's silence. But haven't you ever wondered what the reaction of that same world would have been if . . .? I know, you're going to interrupt me straight away. Israel is not just any State. It's a refuge for the descendants of those who lost their lives simply because of the fact that they were Jews. I've never claimed the contrary. But I've always considered that the victims of one of the most agonizing dramas in modern history had an obligation, if not a duty, to transcend the values of mankind and make sure that others' lives were never put in danger. In fact, one is driven to the conclusion that the very opposite has happened. Not only is the State of Israel scattering death in its wake, but the Jews are giving it their moral support to do so.

When I say 'the Jews', I of course exclude the minority who have, so far, dared to dissent from this deadly policy. And I also make an immediate exception of all those who came and swelled the ranks of the great protest demonstration after the Sabra and Shatila massacres in 1982 . . .

I want to turn now to a more specifically political theme, in order to show you how certain myths maintained by the Jews, myths that die hard, will lead them sooner or later to the edge of the abyss.

You often, in our conversations, raised the question of Israel's security. Each time, I replied that that was no longer an important aspect, and that an extra piece of territory, some fifty kilometres wide, would not stop a modern army from reaching the shores of the Mediterranean.

The examples are many: not least in Israel's own military experience. The punitive raids it has carried out over a radius of two thousand kilometres, from Africa to Mesopotamia, in the space of a few hours, have shattered for ever the traditional theories of waging war.

I'm not taken in, my friend. You spoke to me of security, but what you were really talking about was the realization of a Biblical dream, the development of a territory that was vital to Israel's economic growth: a *Lebensraum*. Can you imagine?

Israel tried, but it immediately came up against one big problem: the Palestinian territories conquered in 1967 were densely populated, and the population, having learned the lesson of the traumatic exodus of 1948, was not going to let itself be terrorized; this time, it did not abandon the land.

Do you remember my asserting that Israel would never succeed, that times had changed and the Palestinians would resist? You smiled, and said that the Jews, strengthened by the experience of ages, would know the best method to recommend to Israel to get round this difficulty.

Israel resorted to a subterfuge. As the Palestinian population had not fled, it had to be 'absorbed' at all costs, and made a trump card in Israel's economic progress. Here was a cheap labour force that could be exploited, thus making the economy of the occupied territories irreversibly dependent on that of Israel.

But, by an irony of fate, the first obstacle to this policy was, in fact, a product of that very ideology of expansion and annexation. It was the proponents of a 'Greater Israel' who wouldn't play the colonialist game . . . I imagine the word 'colonialist' shocks you. But I insist on calling a spade a spade, and I'm sure you realize that for those involved in this policy, it was certainly a classic colonialist enterprise . . . As I said, they wouldn't play the game, these settlers who came running, from Jewish communities all over the world, as soon as it seemed that the dream was finally attainable. Sustained as they were by a boundless religious fanaticism, these men had in mind a rather different colonialist project: they were settlers, certainly, but they wanted to settle in a virgin land; consequently, the territories had to be progressively emptied. They advocated the use of the old slogan of the Jewish Agency in the Thirties: 'Jewish work for a Jewish land.' The economic aspect was just as important to them, but they boasted that they, and they alone, would be the ones to make the land yield up its produce and contribute to the greater glory of Israel.

There was a second obstacle: the Palestinians, hardened by decades of struggle, would not give way before the settlers' strategy, which became official Israeli policy in 1977, with the rise to power of the great ideologist of 'Eretz Israel', Menahem Begin.

And now? One thing is certain. I state it unequivocally: we won't surrender.

Israel has tried, and is still trying, to colonize us. It will fail. Why not face facts?

Of course, you'll say that Israel can't afford to fail, because its security is at stake. If you really must steer the debate back in that direction, shouldn't you at least take the obsolete argument to its logical conclusion?

For me, one thing is certain. Supposing that Israel, of its own free will, applies the famous Resolution 242 of the UN Security Council and withdraws from the territories it occupied in 1967, in the context of a peace treaty formally signed with its neighbours, the young Palestinian state which comes into being on its borders will be so preoccupied with the tasks facing it and the difficulties attendant on its development that there is no way it could possibly constitute a threat for years to come. And I'll add something else, and you can believe me, my friend: my people, finally gathered together on the soil of its homeland and experiencing the pleasures of a peaceful life after so many years of ceaseless struggle, will have to be vigilant as far as their own security is concerned. Quite frankly, the Palestinians have more reason to be worried about the warlike intentions of Israel, and the rise of a racist and fanatical Jewish fundamentalism, as represented by Kahane, than the Israelis have to be worried about them. For that reason, *we* are the ones who will be sure to demand unshakeable guarantees from the great powers.

Forgive my distrust, but you must realize that we have suffered the consequences of Israel's desire for hegemony for so long now that we will have to remain on our guard, at least for a time.

I know your objection. As you so often told me, the threat to Israel's survival, notwithstanding its current military supremacy, rests in the long term. And you always steered me back to the image of the Jewish island lost in an Arab ocean. I can understand how, for the Jews, this relative isolation leads to a genuine anxiety. And yet you maintained that the choice of an Arab Palestine for the realization of the Jewish destiny, a choice made centuries ago, had been arrived at lucidly and was indeed inevitable, since the Bible itself ordained it. Where is the logic in all that? Unless the founding fathers of Zionism took their desires for reality: didn't they proclaim Palestine a virgin land? But what about the Arab world? Was that virgin, too?

I don't think you can escape this basic contradiction. You can't go on forever calling black white. Sooner or later, you Jews will have to dispel the illusions of your beloved Israel and offer it the chance to become integrated into the region where you chose to establish it; you will have to make it see reason.

To be integrated does not mean to be destroyed, but to be fulfilled.

You Jews must trample the Massada complex underfoot once and for all. If you look at it closely, you will see that, far from being a source of strength, it is, in fact, a confession of weakness.

You must all take your courage in your hands. You'll find us responsive to the least sign.

Rest assured of one thing: the Palestinian people will never be subjugated.

Just look at the human potential of this people and what it stands for, look at its level of education, its culture, its huge contribution to human civilization.

For forty years, you Jews have tried desperately to make the world forget that we existed. You've systematically falsified the history of Palestine, raising distortions to the level of doctrine. You've attempted to mislead everyone, to such an extent and with such success that you yourselves have fallen into your own trap. Didn't you tell me one day that, by wanting so strongly to believe it, you were convinced that Palestine had been 'a land without people for a people without land', as the slogan of the Jewish Agency had declared. That was the basis on which a worldwide strategy of disinformation was built: everyone had to be persuaded that the 'promised land' had been, to all intents and purposes, a wilderness for two thousand years, awaiting the return of the Jews.

This indoctrination even affected your own memory. The coast, from Ras-el-Naqura to Gaza, strewn with orange groves planted and lovingly tended by generations of Palestinians, became, in your imagination, strangely sandy; the hills of Galilee, where apple trees, peach trees, apricot trees blossomed every spring, became dry and stony; the olive groves on the outskirts of our towns and villages seemed to you, brainwashed as you were by your own propaganda, to have been so many plots of land

47

which the Zionist settlers had reclaimed for cultivation.

Did you really believe, even for a moment, that the rough hands of the Arabs who had tilled the land of Palestine, who had sowed the crops, grafted the plum trees, pruned the fig trees, lopped the branches off the lemon trees, trimmed the vines, that these hands could ever forget; or that the scent of the orange blossom could ever be obliterated from our collective memory?

And I'll tell you this: the hills of Palestine would have been more verdant, its gardens more resplendent, its cities more thriving, if the sweat of Arab and Jewish brows had mingled; if you Jews had been clear-sighted enough to spare this sacred land from being soaked with the blood of its children.

How disappointed I am, my friend! Yes, I've returned to the subject of your unbearable silence. Please don't be offended: it's just that I can't get used to it.

Are there gaps in your conscience now? Large empty spaces? Vast, arid stretches of desert, like those that infiltrate the conscience of every man who refuses to acknowledge that the task of History is to heal?

What I'm saying is that self-interest sometimes triumphs over solidarity, and that those who

49

succumb to it are throwing the accumulated suffering of mankind into a huge black hole, where they hope the centrifugal force of destruction will grind it into dust.

It can't be done. I'm telling you that, as the eternal optimist that I am. You often criticized me for this attitude, and told me that I was an incredible idealist. For you, such optimism was an illusion, as long as men still wanted to crush their fellow men, as long as revolutions continued to devour their children.

But I still cling to it. I still have a profound faith in mankind, I still believe its highest values can never be debased. Some have tried, others follow suit from time to time, but I remain convinced that these are nothing but passing episodes, aberrations, rather than part of the natural course of human conduct.

The conscience of Man can never, by definition, be completely suppressed. Flaws may appear in it, but not enough to obscure or destroy it. I invite you to join me, and together we can mend these faults.

Your conscience can never self-destruct, despite all your efforts. It's a fine conscience; I've known it well.

That's why I find your silence intolerable.

I find myself all at once thinking about clarity of vision, and wondering if it's a virtue of which every man is capable.

Please don't think I'm being conceited or complacent when I say that. I don't claim to hold the secret of this faculty which enables a man, at a particular moment of his life, to determine exactly the right course to take. Nevertheless, the first time I met you, I felt myself invested with such clarity of mind that I was able, without a moment's hesitation, to see where the essence of my mission lay: in working towards bringing closer the inevitable moment of coexistence.

At this stage, it seems to me imperative that you show a similar clarity and acknowledge that we Palestinians regard the PLO as our only legitimate voice, the only representative of our hopes and aspirations.

I can already hear the word 'never' forming on your lips, that absurd word which causes so many misunderstandings and which is both an automatic knee-jerk reaction and part of a deliberate policy of burying your head in the sand.

How much longer will you carry on rejecting the truth that is staring you in the face?

If today we are in a position to formulate a coherent policy, a vision of the future, to gather our people throughout the diaspora (the Palestinian diaspora this time), to channel its creative energies, shape its fight for freedom

53

and propose peace, it's thanks to a handful of men who have been able to inspire us with the will to forge our future through sacrifice. These men have never forgotten the words of the famous poet Abul-Qassem al-Shabi: 'Once a people desires to live, then Destiny cannot but grant its wish.'

How much longer will you continue with this cynical blindness which deprives you of your usual powers of perception?

I used to challenge you to look me straight in the face whenever you came out with that almost automatic litany of reasons why you refused to deal with those designated as the spokesmen of the Palestinian people. It was because I wanted to see through that impenetrable façade, I wanted to tear aside that veil; I was incensed by all those years of denial, denial not only of Palestinian institutions but of the very right of an Arab people to exist in a land where Israel had taken root.

Never, as long as the PLO hasn't renounced terrorism, do you say?

I won't let myself be dragged into another dialogue of the deaf on that subject. But let me just refresh your memory: when young Palestinians were buried alive by a bulldozer, or when a car with all its passengers was crushed by a tank, in both cases the drivers of these deadly vehicles were Israelis.

'Which hand do you write with?' asked the officer.

'The right hand,' replied the teenager.

'Which of you is good enough at karate to break his right hand?' the officer asked his men.

The officer was an Israeli, the teenager a Palestinian.

Oh, but of course, I almost forgot . . .

Whatever the circumstances, the wolf is always Palestinian, and the lamb always Israeli. Never mind that the lamb – many miles away from the one in the fable – is able to deploy an arsenal consisting of thousands of tanks and fighter aircraft, the wolf still manages to terrorize him with a few stones. I find it hard to believe that you could ever have maintained this argument, or that today, following this logic, and echoing that Israeli commander who recommends beatings against Palestinian youths, you could declare that 'nobody dies' from a few broken limbs.

I hope I'm wrong, my friend. I hope you've changed your point of view, and that you sometimes think of us as human beings, with a natural desire to be treated with respect, and equally natural feelings of national pride.

And I can only reiterate my deep loathing of all acts of violence. As you know, I'm one of those who believe that the Biblical law of 'an eye for an eye and a tooth for a tooth' is immoral; it can be avoided, but for that to happen, man must immediately renounce all aggression against his fellow man.

Every act of violence is a terrorist act because it strikes terror. One can't weigh terror by two different systems of measurement. Israeli bombing raids cause as much terror to Palestinian children as do hails of machine-gun fire from Palestine guerillas to Israeli children.

But as long as Israel hasn't renounced its plans for hegemony and its desire to crush the Palestinian people by force of arms, the latter has no choice but to defend itself.

Tell the men who control the destiny of Israel to swap the little Arabic phrase book used by the Israeli military, its pages full of terrifying expressions of hate, for a document on which the word PEACE is written in capital letters.

Don't be afraid to give this advice. You can't lose by it.

There's a word that has continued to haunt me since we stopped seeing each other, a word which was the subject of the most heated argument we had in the course of our long friendship. It was the word 'reprisals', which you used whenever the Israeli army attacked a refugee camp, and which I could never accept.

The only reason I want to stir up this old debate, even if it causes dissension, is that, today more than ever, I think it's necessary to lance this abscess and find some common ground between us. As you yourself observed one day, I don't contest certain historical facts, nor do I try to confuse different situations experienced by the Palestinians and the Jews, even when their tragedies can in many ways be compared.

My friend, it's certainly possible to throw dust in people's eyes for quite a long time, especially if one occupies a position of strength and controls certain means of communication. But not indefinitely. There's surely something deceitful about using the word 'reprisals' every time the Israeli army (I suppose you still call it *Tsahal*, with an air of smugness?) razes a Palestinian village or camp to the ground. It's a way of deliberately confusing the roles of the two parties. For there to be 'reprisals', there must have been a previous act of aggression, in which case one would have to go back through the whole cycle of violence to find the initial action that set it off.

I know your answer: the Arabs attacked the nascent Jewish state and tried to annihilate it.

But I'd like us to take a closer look at the origins of that hostile act.

My grandfather used to tell me how, around the beginning of this century, the Palestinian Arabs began to be aware that the increasingly frequent waves of Jewish immigrants arriving in the country were not prompted by a spirit of coexistence, but on the contrary, by a quite obvious animosity towards them. Some, annoyed at the presence of this native population in a supposedly uninhabited land, embarked on a campaign of harassment to force it to leave. Others saw in it a valuable labour force, at least at the beginning.

As you see, things haven't changed. The situation is still the same: there are still two styles of colonization for a land that didn't belong to the Jews . . . Don't scream! The owners of this land were Arabs. Legally, the Jews had no right to it. If the spiritual appeal of the land made immigration inevitable, they should have gone about it in a different way. If they wanted the existing inhabitants to accept them, they should have made it quite clear that they were willing to live in peace with them. They could hardly expect the Arabs to welcome them with open arms when they made no secret of their intention to drive them from their lands!

The settlers used every means at their disposal, from coercion to negotiating with the often absentee feudal landowners . . . I can see your sardonic smile . . . It wasn't the Jews' fault if the feudal landowners sold them their lands. That way they became legal owners of Palestine. Now it's my turn to be indignant! You're incorrigible! Owners of Palestine?

Definitely not, my friend. The figures are indisputable. When the State of Israel was proclaimed in 1948, the Jews owned just 5.66% of the land, while the rest belonged to the Arabs . . . Do you contest the figures? . . . I assure you I haven't invented them: they're included in the official documents of the UN General Assembly.

All the property and belongings of the Palestinians were seized by Israel that year. Whole towns – Nazareth, Acre, Jaffa, Haifa, Ramleh, Beisan – as well as the Arab quarters of Tiberias, Safad and the New City of Jerusalem. More than eight hundred villages. All the land outside the urban conurbations. Entire businesses, both commercial and industrial, with all their fixtures and fittings, their supplies, their merchandise. About seven thousand shops and offices. Furniture, personal effects, cash, carpets, paintings and *objets d'art*.

The Jews, encouraged by the flight of the Arabs, set about their enterprise of plunder on such a scale that David Ben-Gurion himself later admitted how ashamed and distressed he had been at this spectacle of unbridled vandalism.

The body responsible for looking after the property of those who had fled presented a report to the Knesset on 18 April 1949, in which it justified these acts with the argument that the Arabs had presented 'the victors of the combat with serious material temptations' by leaving such an enormous amount behind!

You have to admit that this argument, though certainly original, is quite shocking. It's the first time, to my knowledge, that the concept of *temptation* appears as a legal defence. It's usually employed as an extenuating circumstance in criminal cases, but never as an excuse for a crime!

My family was among the victims. I'll never forget my father taking a last look at our house, carefully locking the door and putting the keys in his pocket.

It was at the end of the last century that the Zionist movement began to cast covetous eyes on our lands; and since then, we've paid the price for the establishment of the Jews in Palestine. We've paid a high price: exile, suffering, bloodshed. And despite all that, Israel claims to be the victim and makes the Palestinians out to be its persecutors.

You admitted to me one day that you understood how grave an injustice had befallen the Palestinians, but that there was no other solution for the millions of Jews who had survived the Nazi genocide. That's a spurious argument, and you know it. The Jews in Palestine had a clear plan of action, which they began to put into practice as long ago as the turn of the century: to force the Arabs to leave, by terror if need be. The reason the relationship between the two communities had reached breaking-point by 1948 was that the Jews had never made any secret of their intention to seize the country for themselves. There were a few rare souls among the settlers who demonstrated a desire to live in peace with the Arabs, and not to take their place. And these few men and women of goodwill were soon denounced and ostracized by the Jewish community.

Let's get back to that argument of yours: that the injustice suffered by the Palestinians was justified by the Nazi genocide of the Jews. But isn't it inconceivable that the victims of one of the great injustices of History should then turn round and demand its pound of flesh from a peace-loving people?

And since the word 'genocide' has reared its head, I'd like to bring our differences right out in the open once more. Don't worry, I won't use a dictionary.

And I'm certainly not trying to minimize or relativize the genocide of the Jews by bringing up this question.

What I disputed in those days was how selective you were. As if death were able to claim only certain people, and not others!

According to you, the word 'genocide' could be applied only to the slaughter of the Jews. But what is one to call, for example, the fate of the Armenians at the beginning of this century? Weren't a large percentage of them put to the sword? Wasn't that genocide, in the strict sense of the term?

The Armenians come naturally to mind, because a good many of them sought refuge in Palestine, and have lived on good terms with the Arabs ever since. And our mutual friend Vahé took my side when we quarrelled about the meaning of the word 'genocide'. He also found it difficult to accept the restrictions you wanted to impose, especially after he had given you a detailed description of those terrible years during which the Armenians were decimated.

I remember how, under pressure from Vahé, you finally conceded the point: 'Well, why not . . . in the last analysis . . . maybe for the Armenians.' And then you turned belligerently to me: 'Don't regard that as any kind of concession to you. First of all, your Arab brothers have killed a hundred times more Palestinians than Israel has during its years of struggle, and secondly . . . secondly . . . well, it's not the same thing.'

You were stammering because you weren't convinced by what you were saying, and because your conscience was uneasy. The previous day, in response to your scathing attack on me after a Palestinian bomb had cost the lives of two Israeli children – an unjustifiable action I strongly condemned – I had run through a list of Israel's many acts of violence. The Palestinian victims could be numbered in tens of thousands. You seemed so astonished that I had the impression you had been caught off your guard. I don't think you had ever realized the extent of the slaughter. When you regained your composure, you retorted caustically: 'For there to be genocide, there has to be a premeditated intention to exterminate a whole community, a whole people, a whole race.'

There's no doubt there has to be an explicit intention. But isn't Israel's intention with regard to the Palestinians explicit? Israel denies the Palestinian people's right even to exist. And stemming from that denial there has been a systematic campaign to wipe it off the face of the earth. Couldn't that *also* lead to genocide?

The campaign is not, of course, a massive one; it's not concentrated in time; it's constant, methodical, organized, and spread out over many years.

But this isn't a semantic quarrel. Use whatever terminology you like. The facts are clear. They're written in blood . . .

And yet the exceptional suffering of the Jews ought to have made them wiser and more enlightened.

I'd say that, as a result of their suffering, they ought to have been able to escape being fatally drawn into the pitiless struggle of man against man.

I refuse to believe that they've blotted out the memory of their own past. By turning their backs on the suffering of others, worse still, by causing it themselves, they've automatically

70

failed the test of History, the test at which the torture victim ought to outshine everyone else.

My friend, Israel has failed in the very area where the Jews ought to have helped it to succeed.

You bear the responsibility for that.

The main reason why Israel is now sinking into the abyss, where it will join the sinister brotherhood of nations that show no mercy, is that you placed it above suspicion and showed such complacency towards its leaders.

I promised I would tell you what I really thought. I have no reason to spare you in your silent retreat. You, more than anyone, have a moral duty that you can't escape.

Don't be angry with me. I'm using this tone with you because in the past you constantly told me that you hoped that I would be your *alter ego*.

71

I shared that hope. It was a beautiful dream, and you have no right to turn away from it. The time has come to bring it to fruition.

I'm still daring to hope that you'll soon abandon your silence, relieve me of my pain, and stop Israel's deadly campaign against my people.

Didn't you tell me that you had managed to understand my anxiety just as I had grasped yours? You even swore you would protect me if I were in danger.

Your voice today will help me.

I've wept for your dead. Now weep for mine.

No, the problem isn't insoluble, and it isn't only force that will settle it. Whenever you asked me point-blank: 'Do you deny the existence of a Jewish nation?' and then, without a break: 'Its right to the land of Palestine?' you were thinking in terms of power.

There was a time when I would have reacted impulsively to such words. That time is past. The emotionalism of the Arabs has been exploited often enough for the Palestinians to have learned their lesson.

My position is still clear: there are other avenues to explore in order to arrive at a settlement. An embryonic solution already exists in the willingness of the Palestinians to live in peace with those Israelis who *express the same wish*. All the forces of destruction in the world won't be able to break that determination if it's sincere on both sides.

The Jewish communities around the world would certainly place Israel in a bad position if they persisted in advising it to resort to force to overcome the Palestinian resistance.

We'll never let ourselves be demoralized, or degraded, or intimidated. Never.

And then, this argument about the existence of a Jewish people is so sterile! Even though I told you I didn't deny the existence of any people from the moment it declared itself as such, you kept coming back to the same refrain.

You'll notice that, in this case, I'm not afraid

to accept the evidence. I grant you, without question, what you've always demanded of me. Now it's up to you to take a step towards me and acknowledge the validity of my grievances.

Shout it out loud and clear: the Palestinian nation exists, and it has a right to self-determination on the soil of its homeland.

However, I want to come back to the notion of the right of the Jews to the land of Palestine. Don't worry, I'll spare you the 'by what right?', 'by whose wish?' of our initial encounters. Nor will I make any comment on the astonishing words uttered by Golda Meir on 15 October 1971: 'This country exists as the result of a promise made by God Himself. It would be absurd to ask for its legitimacy to be recognized.'

Let me be clear. I accept that the Jews have a religious aspiration to live in the land of Palestine, but I want to remind you of the morality of the question. I don't intend to go into all the historical and legal ramifications, but all the same, I want to draw your attention to the fact that for the past two thousand years, that period crucial to the claims of the Jews, Palestine has been inhabited.

My family, which is Christian, can trace its family tree for several centuries. Some people we know could find ancestors among the generation of Christ's apostles. Others could go back to the year of the Prophet Mohammed's nocturnal visit (*Al-Isra'*) to Jerusalem. My grandfather, whose grave is today covered with undergrowth on a slope of Mount Zion, used to tell me with pride that the records of our church still contained certificates of births, baptisms, marriages and deaths dating back more than two centuries . . .

The Jews weren't unaware that we were attached to our land. Yet they didn't hesitate to uproot us in the name of their Biblical right.

You'll reply that the Jews were themselves

hounded throughout an old Europe rife with anti-Semitism, and that they had no choice. That was true in the Thirties, with the rise of Nazism, and, to a lesser extent, just after the First World War. But the first waves of immigrants swept Palestine well before those dates. The first Jews landed in Palestine in the second half of the nineteenth century and immediately undertook to colonize the country. They were realizing a dream, the dream of the 'return to Zion'.

They noticed that the Palestinians existed. But the first Zionist Congress, held in Basle in 1897, deliberately refused to recognize the fact. That refusal is still the official line of the State of Israel today. When Levi Eshkol was asked, a few days before he died, whether he thought that the Palestinians also had a right to a homeland, he exclaimed: 'What's a Palestinian? . . . Palestine was a desert inhabited by a few Arabs and Bedouins.' Those shameful words still echo in my ears, as do those of Golda Meir: 'There's no such thing as a Palestinian . . . They don't exist . . .'

Please try to understand. I'm not hostile to the idea that the Jews claim Palestine as the birthplace of their religion. In that case, the notion of a historical right is more a matter of the emotional bond that every Jew feels with the land of Palestine than of any legal concept. What would happen to the world if everyone used that notion as an argument for his own claim to such and such a territory?

I quite deliberately accept that the Jews can live in the land that they evoke in their prayers, but on the condition that they live together with its genuine inhabitants, those who tilled its fields and made its deserts bloom.

No right allows people to deprive others of their birthright, even if it's in the name of God and all His prophets.

I've waited years for you to express openly your condemnation of that original sin. I'm still waiting.

The Jews, my friend, aren't infallible, even if they hold fast to the idea that they're 'the chosen people'. A people can't be 'chosen', any more than it can claim to be free, if it acquires its freedom and its 'chosen-ness' at the expense of others. The sufferings that Israel spreads in its wake throughout the 'promised land' call the whole concept into question. The murder of a Palestinian child has compromised it once and for all.

So wake up, shake off your lethargy!

I've looked for your face in the crowd. In vain. It's obvious you're still turned in on yourself, searching for a fleeting security.

Unless the brutality of the Israeli repression, which every day is reaching unprecedented levels, has given you a sense of false security!

Unless you're still clinging to the comfortable role of descendant of a victim of the Nazi torturers . . . Don't be offended! You know my true feelings on that subject. But I do find that your desire to use it as a way of making everyone feel guilty is occasionally exaggerated. You even tried to include me in the multitude of the guilty.

No, I'm not contesting the right of the Jews to blame severely the legions of collaborators or those who stood by indifferently and gave free rein to the infernal Nazi machine. I'm just calling into question your tendency to curse everyone indiscriminately and use that as an excuse to justify Israeli actions against the Palestinians.

Am I being hard? When I see a child shot down because he dared to throw a stone, or a young girl killed in cold blood, I can't help taking a hard line with you.

Forgive me for judging your silence to be one of consent. Prove to me that I'm wrong.

Don't stay behind that wall of silence when human beings are suffering and dying.

It's time to speak the language of the heart. Love my people as I cherish yours. They are fellow creatures. They are brothers.

I won't hide the fact that, since I started writing you these few lines, I, too, have been afraid. I know there are men, on the other side of that wall in Jerusalem where I perched as a child to watch the Israelis, who would like to destroy me because I contradict their vision of the future, because I seek peace.

There are many such people plotting against life. We both attacked them in the past, with their hollow words and their misleading proposals. Their special envoys crisscross the globe, bearing magic formulas as a cover for their underhand schemes.

Only you can put paid to their lethal plans.

I invite you to be brave.

I'm hesitating. Should I talk to you about music? The reason I'm hesitating is that it seems perverse to mention harmony when the relationship between us is so discordant.

Nevertheless, our exchanges in this field were always so fruitful and rewarding in the past that I can't help pursuing this line.

Let's take folk music first. If one listens to the folk music developed by the Israelis, one is forced to observe that it borrows more from Arab music than from any Jewish musical source. True, there are certain Central European 'Yiddish' intonations that appear from time to time in the shape of the melodies or the ebb and flow of the rhythms, but they are fleeting and do not colour the music to any particular extent. When I drew your attention to this fact one day, you replied heatedly that it was an anomaly, a strange diversion from the true path of Jewish inspiration. Do you remember my own opinion? I said that this musical language was a healthy sign, because it was faithful to the image of the society from which it sprang, a society with a majority of Oriental Jews, Sephardim . . . No, I'm not trying to step into any particular rift . . . I just want to repeat that the nostalgic song of the *nay** which hangs in the air of Palestine is irresistible. You want to drive it away, beyond the Jewish horizon; for you, Jewish inspiration can come only from the West, and the music of Israel has to be a reflection of that 'bastion of civilization'.

---

* *Nay*: a kind of flute common in Arab music (translator's note).

Incidentally, hasn't the same thing happened with Israeli food, which, even more than Israeli music, reflects the region? But let's get back to music.

We often talked about the other facet of the art of music, the classical. At the beginning, you felt ill at ease, indeed you were openly embarrassed . . . Am I exaggerating? Hardly. I'll never forget the puzzled expression on your face, or the suspicion in your voice, when I listed for you the great names of classical music, those peerless interpreters Menuhin, Horowitz, Klemperer, Rubinstein. 'All Jews,' you cried, but I could sense another undertone in your words: 'What do you know about such things?' As a Westerner, you were staggered that an Arab could approach a subject that you considered the property of a certain culture, a culture that for you was light years away from that of the Arabs, which you despised.

I reminded you that Art knows no limits, except those set by its great interpreters, including Jews, and cannot bear to be confined within frontiers, and I challenged you to find in the great works of Bartok, or the late Liszt, anything other than a universal inspiration.

You gradually accepted the idea, especially as, little by little, I opened up to you the world of Arab classical music: a music which was never written down, never committed to paper despite numerous efforts, such as those of the great Al-Farabi (who, in the ninth century, wrote a treatise incorporating quarter-tones and eighth-tones into the traditional melodic line), but which was passed on from father to son like a splendid echo of the Arab universe.

In the end, you had to admit that the Arabs, too, could lay claim to artistic traditions going back to the dawn of time.

Whether you wanted to or not, you had to acknowledge that the Arabs, too, could be the descendants of Abraham, Ibrahim al-Khalil.

In the past, you always lost your temper whenever the media emphasized scenes of terror inflicted by Israeli soldiers on the Palestinian population. These scenes showed the true face of the Occupation, but you refused to accept the reality: that Israel is a colonial power, and a state like any other.

In your anxiety, you clung to one single idea: Israel mustn't show any weakness, because it is surrounded by neighbours who would like nothing better than to destroy it. Time and again, I told you that in arguing that way, you were obscuring (consciously, in my opinion) the heart of the matter: the injustice suffered by the Palestinians.

You were behaving as if peace were a real danger for Israel, as if it were scared of the evil spirits that might attack it if the Arab threat were ever to disappear . . . Wait! Let me explain . . . The entity we call Israel contains so many internal contradictions, inherent in its theo-cratic nature, that only the concept of a holy alliance can overcome its inability to form a true nation. Therefore the supposed external threat must be maintained at all costs, to prevent a confrontation with itself.

Naturally, it was convenient, and – forgive me if I drive the point home – it would have been difficult to do otherwise. By evading the root of the conflict, Israel cultivated the role of the weak victim threatened by a horde of blood-thirsty enemies; to do the opposite would have led to a reversal of roles . . . Don't interrupt . . . No, I'm not trying to pass over in silence the overwhelming responsibility of certain Arab regimes who have contributed towards perpetuating the situation. They've also been able to use the Palestinian cause to their own advantage in more ways than one, especially in allowing them to keep their own populations in a state of oppression. For them, the role of bogeyman they've been assigned couldn't have proved more beneficial.

But who would gain from bringing the Palestinian question out into the open? Nobody, except the Palestinians themselves! Let the conflict become an Israeli–Palestinian one, and the world would view Israel in a new light. The role of victim would change sides. Four million Israelis, equipped with the most sophisticated weapons, confronting four million Palestinians, half of them living under the yoke of military occupation, the other half wandering the globe: there's a picture that might disturb the status quo and expose the *de facto* complicity established between Israel and certain other regimes.

It's already happened, my friend. You never believed me when I told you it was inevitable. All the schemes, tricks and intrigues have failed. All it needed was a few stones and the smokescreen evaporated.

The young Palestinian, like David reborn, has allowed the veil to be torn asunder.

The new Goliath is called Israel. If he persists in spreading terror among the Palestinians, David's stone will strike him on the forehead.

The Jews of the whole world have a duty to halt the Israeli war machine, a machine dedicated to the vilest task imaginable: the destruction of the Palestinian aspiration to life.

You alone, my friend, are capable of sounding the alarm. I still have faith in you.

Have human rights become something that Israel can trifle with as it wishes, without fear of censure?

I don't like hasty comparisons. That's why I won't list the acts of violence committed by the Israeli army against Palestinian civilians, a list that would invite comparison with more than one totalitarian regime.

All the same, when I hear a law student at the Hebrew University in Jerusalem brazenly declare that 'it's necessary to give the young

Palestinian demonstrators a good thrashing, because the Arabs understand only the language of force'; when foreign journalists describe a wall stained with blood, again in Jerusalem, a wall against which Israeli soldiers were in the habit of knocking their victims' heads and breaking their limbs; when Israel's Prime Minister, Yitzhak Shamir, protests: 'We don't have permission to kill them, we don't have permission to expel them, we don't have permission to beat them, we wonder what we have the right to do', then I can't help drawing parallels, even with certain racist regimes.

In Israel, the Palestinians are faced with the cynicism and hostility of an occupying power. Their elementary rights, the rights that everyone considers as basic human rights, are systematically violated. From being beaten with rifle butts, all the way up to deportation . . . Don't lose your temper. What other word can be used when a man is taken blindfolded, and with his hands tied behind his back, as far as the border and then ordered to walk straight ahead; when he is banished from the land that gave him birth and where he has always lived? ... All the way up to deportation, then, the law is manipulated by the occupiers to the detriment of the Palestinian population; men and women are at the mercy of teenagers armed to the teeth; Israeli military supremacy knows no bounds.

Fortunately, at this point in the twentieth century, it's become natural to condemn a regime that raises persecution and discrimination to the level of doctrine, and that orders its armed forces to shoot demonstrators on sight, whatever the political ideas on which they pride themselves.

So in the case of Israel, can you define the 'threshold' beyond which you would consider the human rights of the Palestinians to have been violated? I'm waiting impatiently for your answer!

And don't tell me those are just unfortunate mistakes. You know as well as I do that, as a result of decisions taken at government level, formal orders have been given, now as in the past, allowing the Israeli army to use 'all available means' to quell any stirring of revolt on the part of the Palestinian population. All available means, including shooting real bullets into crowds of demonstrators.

And don't tell me that the human rights of the Palestinians aren't respected by certain Arab governments either. That's no excuse. It would be quite outrageous to hide behind other massacres suffered by the Palestinians.

In Israel, human rights apply only to Jews!

Are they merely an instrument in the hands of the Israeli leaders, who constantly refer to them but only ever implement them in a discriminatory manner?

I leave you to ponder over that.

No doubt many Palestinians will die before the

world judges Israel according to the standards used with regard to every other state in the world.

Our martyrs, killed by a generation of Israeli Jews that has only tenuous links with the generation that knew the agony of torture and death, will join the list of victims of a global holocaust uniting Arabs and Jews, Africans, Asians and Native Americans, all sacrificed to satisfy the hatred that certain men feel for their brothers.

You are, I'm convinced, gradually discovering the unpalatable truth: that Israel is a country made arrogant by conquest and heading rapidly out of control.

More than any speech, the image of that hospital in Gaza, full to bursting with maimed teenagers, can't have left you unmoved.

I'm positive of that because, even at this distance, I can sense the turmoil your conscience is going through.

The day will come when a new generation of Israelis arises.

These Israelis will never have detected the slightest feeling of shame or guilt in their parents. They will be condemned to confront for themselves the depth of this guilt, when they discover that their fathers were killers, or that they are living in houses confiscated from deportees.

This new generation will consider itself a victim of its parents.

Some of its members are already in the streets of Tel Aviv.

Why do you disregard them?

Why don't you encourage the man who dares to say, with a heavy heart: 'The more I break the bones of other people, the more I destroy myself'?

By your silence, aren't you taking the side of the murderers?